Author:

Jacqueline Morley studied English at Oxford University. She has taught English and History and is the author of numerous books, including award-winning historical non-fiction titles for children.

Illustrator:

Mark Peppé studied painting and etching at the Slade School, London. He has been a freelance illustrator since 1962 and has also taught illustration at Eastbourne College of Art. He lives and works in East Sussex.

Series creator:

David Salariya is an illustrator, designer and author. He is the founder of the Salariya Book Company, which specialises in the creation and publication of books for young people, from babies to teenagers, under its imprints 'Book House' and 'Scribblers'.

Editor: **Karen Barker Smith**

Editorial Assistant: **Michael Ford**

First published in hardback in Great Britain
in MCMXCVI by
Book House, an imprint of
The Salariya Book Company Ltd
25 Marlborough Place, Brighton BN1 1UB

SALARIYA

Visit our website at **www.book-house.co.uk**
or go to **www.salariya.com**
for **free** electronic versions of:
You Wouldn't Want to be an Egyptian Mummy!
You Wouldn't Want to be a Roman Gladiator!
Avoid Joining Shackleton's Polar Expedition!
Avoid Sailing on a 19th-Century Whaling Ship!

ISBN 978-1-906714-93-2

A CIP catalogue record for this book is available
from the British Library.

Printed and bound in China.

CONTENTS

A Renaissance Town

Written by
Jacqueline Morley

Series created by
David Salariya

Illustrated by
Mark Peppé

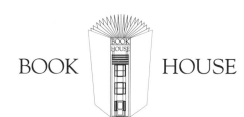

BOOK HOUSE

INTRODUCTION

'Renaissance' is a French word meaning 'rebirth'. The 19th-century French historian, Jules Michelet, used it to describe a new age that banished the medieval world in Europe, and it was such a good name that it has been used ever since. Some great changes, like wars or migrations of peoples, are actions; others, like religious conversions, occur in people's minds. The Renaissance was this second sort of event: a change in people's way of thinking about the natural world, about human beings and about art. The change was caused by the rediscovery of ideas that had been rejected by the Christian Church and forgotten for centuries – the philosophy, poetry and art of the civilisations of ancient Greece and Rome, the so-called 'classical' world.

This 'renaissance' of classical ideas began in Italy among scholars, poets and artists. In the 14th century the Italian poet Petrarch (1304–1374) had collected and studied classical texts, but the great outburst of discussion and enthusiasm began in the 15th century. The place where it all started was the town of Florence in central Italy.

If you had been living in Florence at that time, would you have noticed anything out of the ordinary? This book looks inside the town to find out what went on.

THE TOWN

This is Florence in the 15th century. At that time Italy was not a united country but a collection of independent states. Medieval trade, which was centred on the Mediterranean, had made many Italian towns so prosperous that they had been able to throw off their feudal overlords and become self-governing.

Each of these towns controlled the land around it, and, if it could, it took over weaker towns. Florence, in the central region of Tuscany, was one of the most powerful. Its wealth came from manufacturing high-quality woollen and silk cloth. In the 15th century it had over 50,000 inhabitants. Few other towns were so large and so rich.

This view of Florence is based on a picture map of about 1470. It shows impressive churches and civic buildings, some old, some new, rising above tightly packed medieval houses. The cathedral's huge dome dominates them all.

This 15th-century stone lion stands in the main square. It is the town's emblem.

Florence stands on the banks of the river Arno, about 80 kilometres from the sea. This was an excellent trading position where routes from the north, coming down from the Apennine mountains, met traffic from the port of Pisa at the Arno's mouth. The Etruscans had found in it a good place for a settlement in the 8th century BC, and so had the Romans, who built a city there.

The encircling walls, set with gates and watch-towers, show that 15th-century Florence was still in many ways a medieval town and needed good defences. But times were changing. Increasingly people felt safe enough to live outside the town's walls. Flourishing farms and the villas of rich citizens dotted the hills, making the countryside part of Florence too.

Florence's wealth came from the river Arno, which was its link with the sea and also the basis of its textile industry. Dyeing and fulling, essential processes in making cloth, used lots of water.

THE SQUARE

The heart of Florence was its main square. On any day of the week its large open space was full of people, many of them hurrying about on official business, for this was where the political affairs of the town were decided. The palace of the governing body – the Signoria – was here. Law courts and police headquarters were close by. The square was the place for anyone wanting to have a word with someone important. It was a meeting point for lawyers, officials and everyone who liked political gossip. Apart from a few young people playing games, the atmosphere was serious. Gambling was forbidden in the square.

Florence was proud of the fact that, unlike most Italians towns, it was a republic. The Signoria was run by nine elected officials called 'priors'. They served for two months, then new priors were chosen at random by drawing citizens' names from four leather bags. The system was meant to stop ambitious men from holding on to power. It was not as democratic as it sounds, as there were all sorts of restrictions on the types of people whose names could go into the bags. The constant elections led to much political talk and secret dealings. Florentines loved discussing politics and the way an ideal society should work. Ideas fascinated them.

The battlemented medieval palace of the Signoria, begun in 1298, dominates the square. From the top of its tower a great bell, known from its deep note as 'la vacca' (the cow), is tolled in times of crisis to call all citizens to the square so that they can decide what should be done.

Next to the palace is an open loggia (arcade), added in the 1370s to provide a dignified setting for the priors to receive ambassadors or watch public events in the square. At other times it offers a shady place to sit, and is where old men gather to talk and watch the world go by.

Palace of the Signoria (or Palazzo Vecchio)

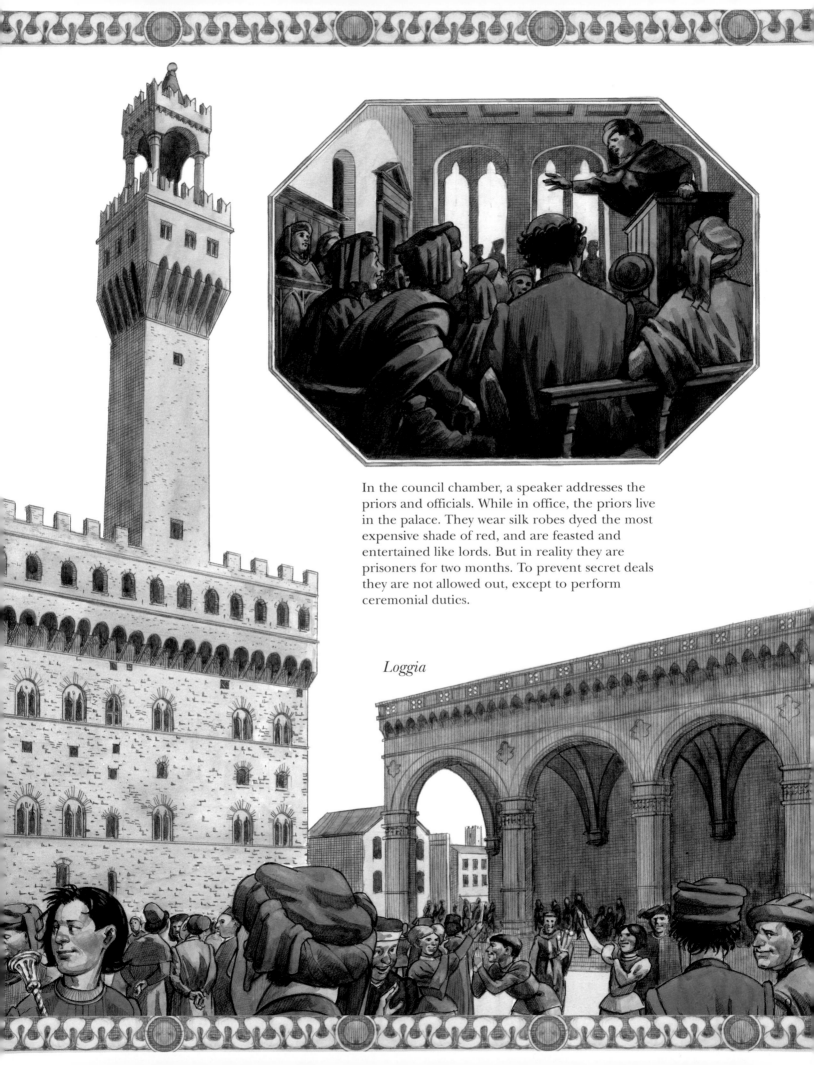

In the council chamber, a speaker addresses the priors and officials. While in office, the priors live in the palace. They wear silk robes dyed the most expensive shade of red, and are feasted and entertained like lords. But in reality they are prisoners for two months. To prevent secret deals they are not allowed out, except to perform ceremonial duties.

Loggia

THE CATHEDRAL

The Florentines' pride in their town's wealth and independence made them willing to spend a great deal on beautifying it. Since the 14th century the Signoria had been using public funds to widen and straighten the crooked medieval streets and enlarge the squares. People also gave money through the guilds, the trade associations to which all skilled workers belonged. The money was spent in the way that everyone thought right: to the glory of God. Religion was the controlling force in people's lives.

In 1296, work had begun on a grand new cathedral planned to hold 30,000 people and to rival the cathedrals of nearby Siena and Pisa. The scheme was organised by the Wool Guild. Its members asked the advice of citizens with specialised knowledge, such as builders, sculptors, painters and goldsmiths, and they even held a referendum (public vote) on the plans. Work went ahead very slowly. The belfry, designed by one of Florence's great painters, Giotto, was begun in 1334 and not finished until 1387, long after his death. By 1471, when the gold ball was set on the top of the lantern, the creation of their magnificent marble-clad cathedral had occupied the hearts and minds of the people of Florence for 175 years.

The winning panel (above) was by a young Florentine goldsmith and sculptor, Lorenzo Ghiberti. He spent 22 years making the doors. He set up a special foundry to cast them, where many craftsmen who became famous later were trained. The runner-up, Filippo Brunelleschi, became a famous architect.

An octagonal baptistery, of the 11th century, faces the cathedral. Florentine babies were brought there to be baptised. In 1401, to give thanks for the town's escape from plague, it was decided that the baptistery should have new bronze doors. The Cloth Merchants' Guild held a competition to decide who should make them. Each contestant was asked to make a bronze panel showing the Bible story of the sacrifice of Isaac.

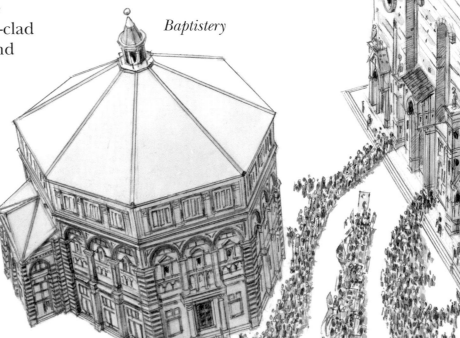

Baptistery

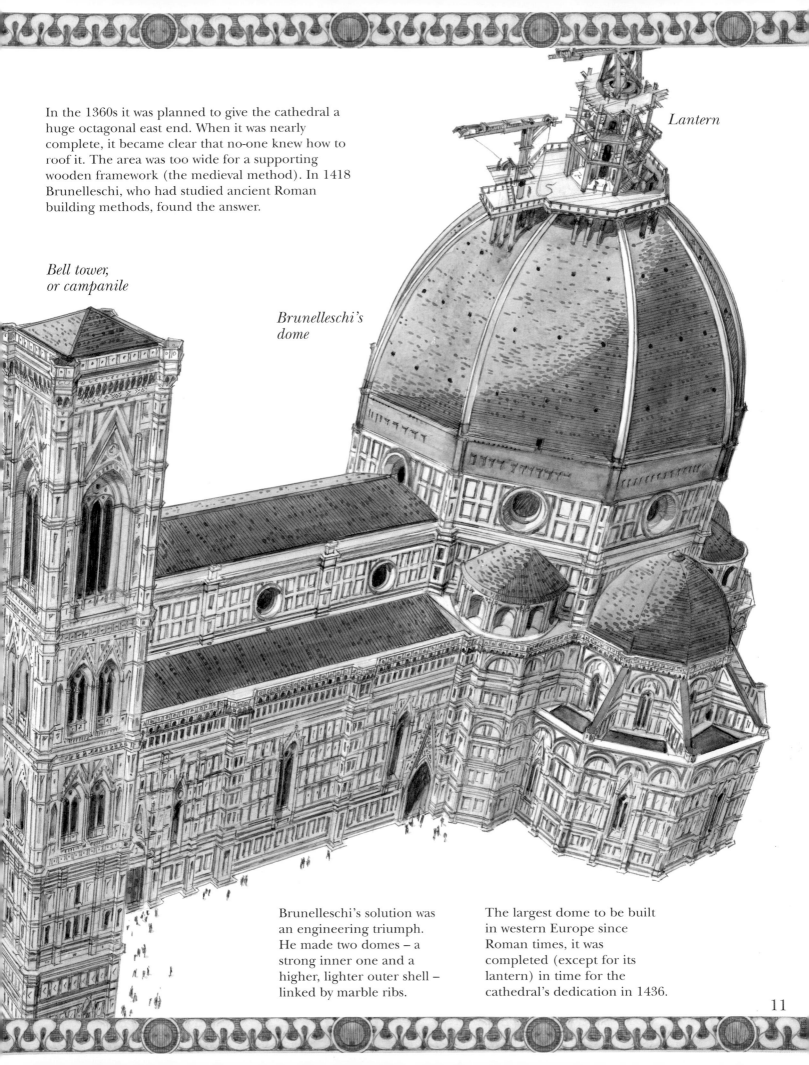

In the 1360s it was planned to give the cathedral a huge octagonal east end. When it was nearly complete, it became clear that no-one knew how to roof it. The area was too wide for a supporting wooden framework (the medieval method). In 1418 Brunelleschi, who had studied ancient Roman building methods, found the answer.

Lantern

Bell tower, or campanile

Brunelleschi's dome

Brunelleschi's solution was an engineering triumph. He made two domes – a strong inner one and a higher, lighter outer shell – linked by marble ribs.

The largest dome to be built in western Europe since Roman times, it was completed (except for its lantern) in time for the cathedral's dedication in 1436.

11

THE MARKET

This is the market square in Florence, always the busiest and most crowded part of town. It is the oldest, too. The forum (main square) of the Roman city was here, and a small settlement that survived the Dark Ages had clustered around this spot. For centuries local farmers, townspeople and travelling traders had met here to buy and sell goods.

Almost everything edible or useful was on sale. Cloth dealers set up their stalls beside apothecaries and cheesemongers, traders in kitchenware, sellers of hawks and falcons, poulterers, vegetable growers, sellers of corn and macaroni, of dried fruit and chestnuts, garlic tarts and herbs fried in batter. Everyone shouted their wares and, through the throng of dealers and buyers, pack animals and loaded carts, the heralds rode calling out news and official announcements.

Donatello's 'Abundance'

In 1428 the town's authorities erected an ancient Roman pillar in the marketplace and asked Florence's most outstanding sculptor, Donatello, to make a statue for it. He sculpted a woman with a basket of fruit on her head and a 'horn of plenty' under her arm to represent 'Abundance' – a good choice for a market. His statue was inspired by ancient Roman figures of the corn goddess, Ceres. At this time no other market in Europe had a statue in this style.

The central building is the meat market, though other trades also used it. The meat market was a 14th-century improvement: a place where meat could be sold in clean conditions, protected from the sun.

The Signoria kept a close eye on the market conditions. In 1415 the butchers were told they would face a fine of 100 lire (quite a large sum) if they did not repair the roof of their covered market within one month.

THE PEOPLE

A noble family. There were many in Florence, and in the past they had caused a lot of trouble with their feuding (fighting).

To keep them out of politics, a law was passed that only guild members could be elected to the Signoria.

A wealthy merchant. Even the richest dressed simply. It was unwise to show off, for envy made rivals into enemies.

His household is with him: his wife, their married son and his family, and behind him some of the servants.

The streets of Renaissance Florence held a rich mixture of people – foreign merchants, pilgrims, scholars and Italians of all kinds, from visiting cardinals to starving crippled beggars. When the city gates opened at dawn, peasants with donkey carts streamed in from the country to unload at the market. Bells began calling people to early Mass and families hurried to church to make a good start to the day. For many women this would be their only outing, since except on festival days, wives and daughters stayed at home to run the household. Women out alone were usually servants, or housewives too poor to afford servants.

Peasant farmers were often in town to buy and sell their goods. They were as much at home there as in the country.

Many people thronging the streets belonged to the church: bishops, nuns, priests, Dominican and Franciscan friars.

There are plenty of young men in Florence. Half the male population is between 14 and 35 years old.

Men married at about 35, so many were free to roam about looking for excitement – a hunt, or a fight with rivals.

This skilled silk-worker is twisting fibres into thread. He is typical of Florence's thousands of craftsmen.

They were the average citizens, not as rich as some merchants, but better off than the unskilled workers.

Many strangers came from afar – Byzantine scholars, pilgrims on their way to Rome, wandering beggars.

Florence was such an important trade centre that merchants with their packhorses came from all over Europe.

The streets soon became busier and noisier, with the blacksmiths' hammering and smoke, the clothmakers' agents scurrying between workshops with wool to be spun or yarn to be woven, the shopkeepers who blocked the roads while they checked deliveries. There were constant shouts from angry carters and warnings that someone important was trying to get by: a visiting lord, a government official, or an ambassador being escorted to the Signoria.

After dark there was a curfew: no-one could be in the streets unless on official business. Late-night revellers slept where they were, rather than risk arrest and a night in the rat-ridden gaol.

Indoors & out

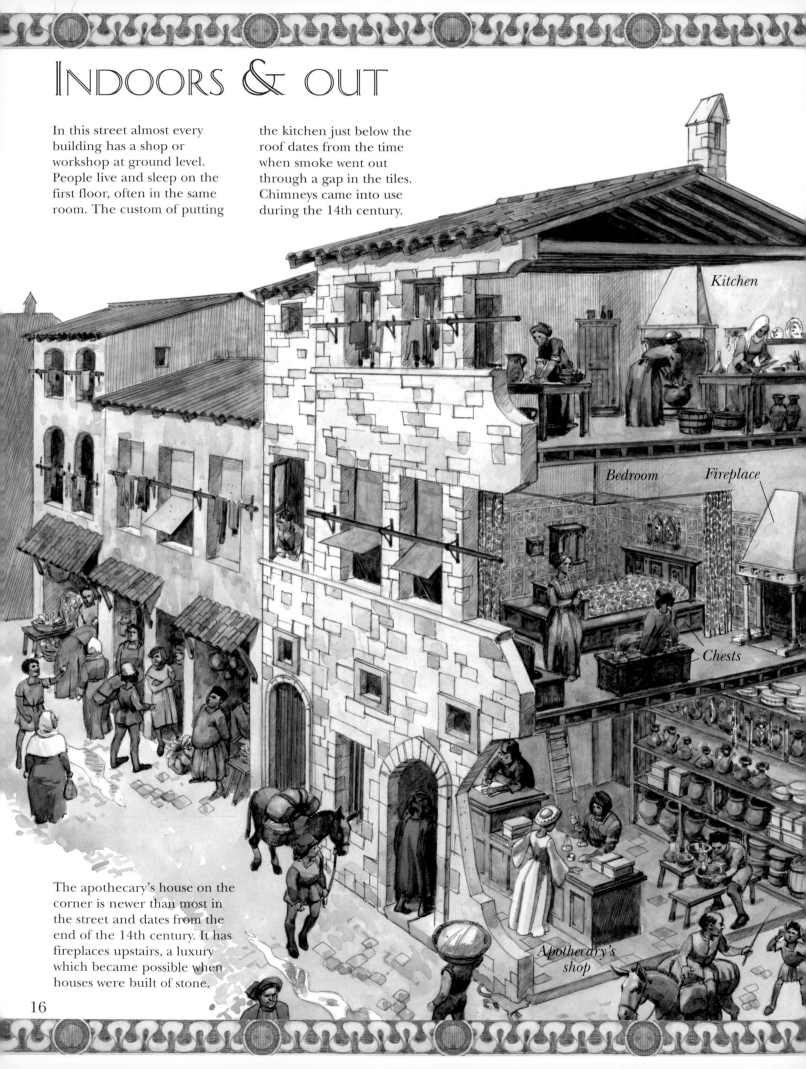

In this street almost every building has a shop or workshop at ground level. People live and sleep on the first floor, often in the same room. The custom of putting the kitchen just below the roof dates from the time when smoke went out through a gap in the tiles. Chimneys came into use during the 14th century.

Kitchen

Bedroom   *Fireplace*

Chests

The apothecary's house on the corner is newer than most in the street and dates from the end of the 14th century. It has fireplaces upstairs, a luxury which became possible when houses were built of stone.

Apothecary's shop

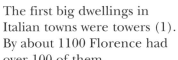

1

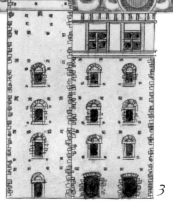

2

3

4

The first big dwellings in Italian towns were towers (1). By about 1100 Florence had over 100 of them.

They were the strongholds of feuding noble clans. Allied families lived in houses near their towers, gradually adding storeys and extra buildings to form a tall block (2) with communicating galleries.

The façades of these forerunners of the *palazzo* (grand family town house) were grim (3). By the 14th century, new houses of this kind had larger windows and regular façades (4).

The corner house is grander than its neighbours, with a rear courtyard and a well. Most people had to get their water from public wells.

Many courtyards had stables and storerooms opening on to the street behind, so that goods did not go through the house. Townspeople who owned a farm could have their own produce sent in to town to be stored.

Although rich merchant families were building themselves fine new homes, most people in 15th-century Florence still lived in old buildings, closely packed into streets like that opposite. Like most of Florence, the street shown here had grown up higgledy-piggledy during the Middle Ages. It is very narrow, and its oldest buildings are wooden. The others have been rebuilt in stone, and are tall, to make the most of the site. This made the lower rooms quite dark. Window glass was still a rarity; oiled cloth stretched on frames, which were hinged to prop open, served instead. At night, heavy wooden shutters covered the windows and the big door to the street was firmly locked and bolted.

Inside, houses were plainly furnished, the walls whitewashed or painted in patterns – sometimes to look like cloth hangings. Even people wealthy enough to have real hangings only put them up for special occasions. Like clothes and linen, they were stored in chests. The most important piece of furniture was the bed. It was made in the room if it would be too big to go through the door. Storage chests were built into it on three sides, and a curtain could be drawn round to make a small private bedroom. Servants slept on trucklebeds, brought out at night.

THE GUILDS

Florence had seven major and fourteen minor guilds in the 15th century. The members of the major guilds – wool manufacturers, silk manufacturers, cloth merchants, bankers, lawyers, furriers, and doctors and apothecaries – were the town's richest businessmen. They controlled the Signoria, although in theory all guild members in Florence had a say in the town's government. (People in the poorest jobs had none, since they were not allowed to form guilds.) Only two of the Signoria's nine priors represented the less wealthy tradesmen of the minor guilds.

GUILD SYMBOLS

The main guilds were active in shaping the town. Their members sat on the committees that planned the cathedral and judged the competition for the baptistery doors. They were tough businessmen but respected craftsmanship. They knew that an expensive piece of work, if of excellent quality, represents good value. When it came to commissioning sculptors to embellish the guild church of Orsanmichele, no costs were spared. Almost every year a new masterpiece was added to the church. By 1450 it had become a display of the wonders of Florentine art.

Silk manufacturers   *Wool manufacturers*

The guilds had their own church, Orsanmichele (below). Begun in 1336, it was originally a grain market with an open arcade all round.

In about 1380 the arches were enclosed, and soon after the guilds made the building their church. Above: guild emblems on the façade.

Each of the richer guilds paid for a statue of its patron saint, to fill fourteen niches on the outside of Orsanmichele. Each guild wanted to be better than the others and commissioned Florence's best sculptors. Six of the statues made between 1406 and 1428 were by Ghiberti or Donatello.

Left: Donatello's St George, made in 1419 for the Armourers' Guild.

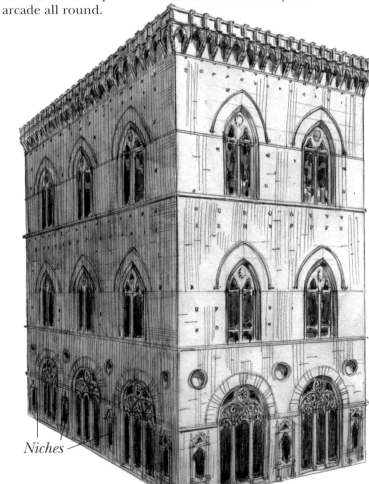

Niches

Each guild laid down rules about materials and standards of craftsmanship which its members had to obey.

This shoemaker is protesting that the leather he uses is well up to the guild's recognised standard.

There were far more than 21 trades in Florence. Several different trades would belong to one guild.

The regulations of the bakers' guild made it the easiest to join, so it was looked down on by the other guilds.

As well as medicines, apothecaries sold herbs, spices, sugar, cosmetics, wax, dyes and pigments for painters.

Painters and gilders belonged to this guild, since they bought many of their materials from the apothecaries.

There was a guild for the sellers of salt, oil and cheese, who were the 15th-century equivalent of modern grocers.

Salt, oil and cheese (and wine) were the basic stores. Most other food was freshly bought or home-made.

The blacksmiths' guild was separate from that of the armourers. No trade could trespass on another's speciality.

The goldsmiths were highly skilled metal-workers. They belonged to the major guild of silk merchants.

The butchers' was the most highly regarded of the minor guilds. Tight rules governed the sale of meat.

Meat was expensive. Veal was thought the healthiest, then pork or lamb. Beef was usually boiled.

WEALTH & POWER

Raw wool was imported from England or Spain. The manufacturers who bought it used overseers to co-ordinate the people who made it into cloth.

First the raw wool was sorted into grades and washed. This was low-paid work done by employees of the wool manufacturer.

Next it was carded (combed) to disentangle and align the fibres, ready for spinning. Most carders were also poorly paid employees.

Women, often country-women, did the spinning at home. The cloth manufacturers' agents brought them the wool and collected the yarn.

Three-quarters of Florentines were cloth workers, many of them poor. Making cloth involved so many people that most of the profit went to those rich enough to finance and organise the whole process, from buying wool to selling cloth. Their close business associates were the international merchants who imported wool and exported cloth and traded in other foreign goods. They might have contacts or agents in France, Spain, Flanders or England. These merchants, who travelled widely and traded on a grand scale, were the most respected people in Florence.

Rich merchants had money to lend, so banking developed with trade. In 15th-century Florence the richest bankers were the Medici family. Giovanni di Bicci de' Medici made the family fortune by becoming banker to the Pope. He died in 1429, leaving a banking empire. His son Cosimo inherited his father's skill and cunning. Without seeming to seek political power, he used his wealth to win allies and crush rivals, so that he controlled the Signoria while apparently only advising it. As a result the Medici family, while in theory remaining private citizens, were really the rulers of Florence.

The 'florin', the gold currency of Florence, bearing the town's emblem, the lily, had been minted since 1252. It was accepted all over Europe because its value did not vary.

The spun thread was wound evenly to prepare it for weaving. Long, equal threads were measured out for the warp (lengthwise threads).

Weavers were men. They worked at home and then delivered the cloth. It took a month to weave an average length of cloth.

The cloth went to the dyers, and then went outside the town to be finished at fulling mills powered by streams that flowed into the Arno.

Dyed and fulled cloth had to be stretched out to dry. It was hung in special drying sheds by the Arno. These kept the sun from fading the dye.

Businessmen discuss a deal (right). The merchant giving some cloth a close inspection is a wealthy importer and exporter. He has just received a new shipment of wool and is selling it to the cloth manufacturer on the left. As part of the deal, the manufacturer hopes to sell him some top-quality finished cloth for export.

Florence was a great banking centre. By the 1420s it had 72 banks. They offered a variety of services: deposit accounts, loans, foreign currency exchange and acceptance of bills of exchange. Florentine merchants invented the 'bill of exchange', a letter which authorised money to be issued in one country and the debt repaid in another, on presentation of the 'bill'. This enabled merchants in different parts of Europe to make deals with each other without having to transfer heavy coins (paper money was unknown in Europe).

New Ideas

Giovanni di Bicci de' Medici owned only three books in 1418. His son Cosimo, another hard-headed merchant, collected thousands (each hand-copied, as all books were then). Why had books become so much more important in such a short time? The reasons go back to the 14th century, when the Italian poet Petrarch became fascinated by ancient Roman writers, collecting their works and discussing them with friends. This new enthusiasm inspired Florentine scholars in the 15th century to hunt out ancient manuscripts decaying in monastic libraries. They discovered in them ideas that the Christian Church had rejected long ago as pagan and misguided. Such scholars were called 'humanists'. Several were friends of Cosimo, who admired their learning, funded their studies and bought all the rare books his agents could discover.

What most excited the humanists was the open-mindedness of classical thought. The Church taught that knowledge was revealed by God; people could discover nothing by their own efforts. But classical thinkers had believed in the ability of humans to examine the world and discover new truths. This gave 15th-century scholars and artists the confidence to think and work experimentally.

The excitement of finding new works and unknown authors was intense. Copies of classical literature survived by the merest chance. The humanists hunted for them in Italy, Germany, Switzerland and France, copying any that were not for sale.

In 1439, Greek-speaking scholars from Byzantium came to Florence as part of a Church delegation (left). Florentines seized the opportunity to study Greek and invited them to lecture at the university. Cosimo de' Medici attended lectures on the philosophy of Plato and decided to form an 'Academy' like Plato's: a group of scholars who would meet to discuss philosophy.

Cosimo educated a poor student, Marsilio Ficino, who became a noted Greek scholar and created Cosimo's own Academy.

Lorenzo

Ficino

Here at the Medici Villa at Carreggi, in around 1490, Cosimo's grandson, Lorenzo (left) listens as Ficino (centre) and other friends exchange ideas.

Lorenzo was now head of the Medici family, and the most powerful man in Florence. He was also a poet and the centre of a brilliant circle of artists and scholars.

Designs for capitals (tops of columns), from a portfolio of drawings by an unknown artist, *c*.1470. Some were copies of classical ones, and some, like these, were fanciful inventions of his own.

The musicians and dancers (right) are the work of the Florentine sculptor, Luca della Robbia (1400–1482), who was influenced by ancient Roman art. They decorate the cathedral's choirloft.

A visitor who explored the ruins in the 1490s to copy Roman paintings wrote about it.

You must go with a guide, he said, and take torches and a picnic of bread, wine and salami.

He scraped his knees on the stones, and was frightened by the snakes, owls, bats and toads.

DIGGING UP THE PAST

The humanists' excitement about the classical world was soon shared by artists. If scholars could learn so much from old books, artists could surely learn from ancient art. Shortly after 1401, two young Florentines, the sculptor Donatello and the architect Brunelleschi, went to Rome. The vast and splendid city of ancient times was now a shabby country town, half the size of Florence.

The ancient Roman ruins lay half buried and overgrown with trees and bushes. The two artists drew sculpted reliefs and measured cornices, columns and vaults to learn how the Romans had created buildings that were still so impressive. Their workmen dug wherever projecting fragments suggested something exciting might lie below. At first people thought they were treasure-hunting.

On their return to Florence, Donatello and Brunelleschi used their knowledge of Roman work to experiment on their own. The impact on their fellow artists was dramatic. Later in the century the fame of Florentine artists was such that they were summoned by the Popes to make Rome beautiful once more.

A NEW PALAZZO

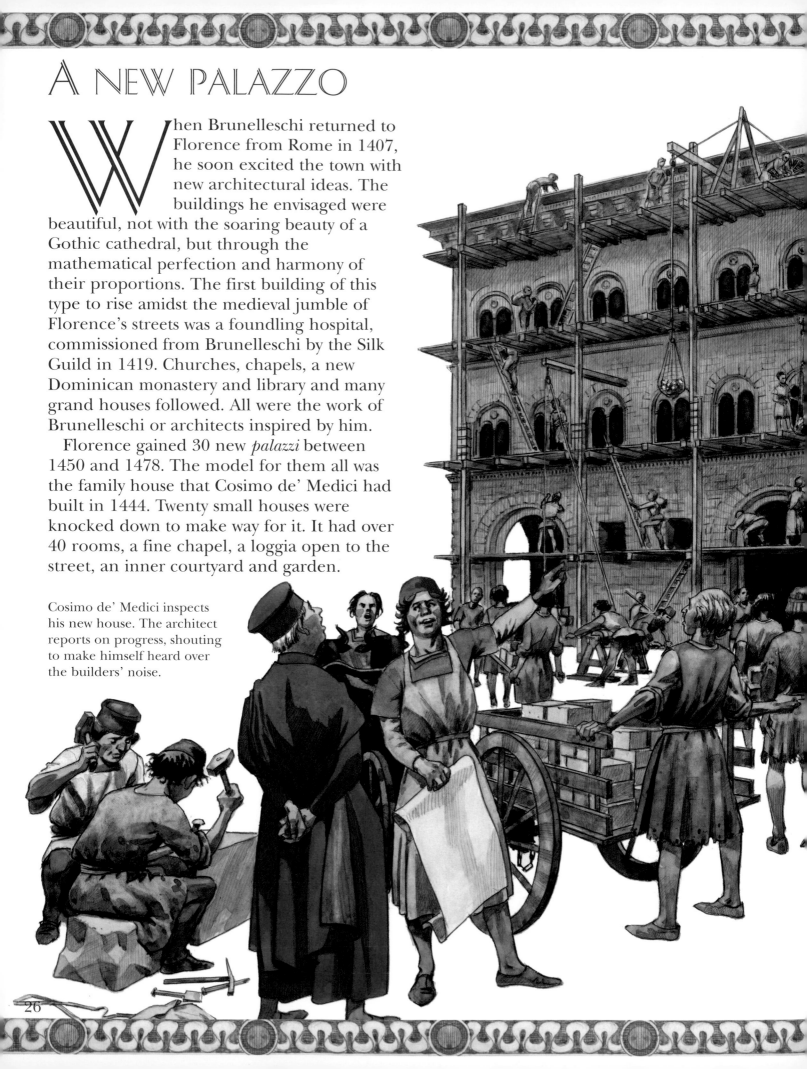

When Brunelleschi returned to Florence from Rome in 1407, he soon excited the town with new architectural ideas. The buildings he envisaged were beautiful, not with the soaring beauty of a Gothic cathedral, but through the mathematical perfection and harmony of their proportions. The first building of this type to rise amidst the medieval jumble of Florence's streets was a foundling hospital, commissioned from Brunelleschi by the Silk Guild in 1419. Churches, chapels, a new Dominican monastery and library and many grand houses followed. All were the work of Brunelleschi or architects inspired by him.

Florence gained 30 new *palazzi* between 1450 and 1478. The model for them all was the family house that Cosimo de' Medici had built in 1444. Twenty small houses were knocked down to make way for it. It had over 40 rooms, a fine chapel, a loggia open to the street, an inner courtyard and garden.

Cosimo de' Medici inspects his new house. The architect reports on progress, shouting to make himself heard over the builders' noise.

To design his new house, Cosimo chose Michelozzo, an architect and sculptor who had been Donatello's pupil.

The façade is ordered and spacious, but still has the fortress-like air of Florence's large medieval houses.

The building is arranged around a courtyard, and follows the classical ideas of order, symmetry and proportion.

The courtyard housed the Medicis' collection of Roman sarcophagi, busts and medallions – the first classical museum.

Florentines were proud of their town's new look, but they grumbled, as people always do, about the building mess. Shopkeepers complained of the constant dust and blocked streets.

Interior decoration soon followed the fashion and took on a classical look. The room on the right, from a painting of the 1480s, has a painted frieze that imitates a sculpted classical relief.

Sculpture old & new

It was one of the luckiest accidents in history that just as the humanists were forming the tastes of Florence's wealthy merchants, the town was producing artists of genius for them to employ. We call them artists now, but in the early 15th century architects, sculptors and painters were regarded as craftsmen no grander than masons or carpenters. Brunelleschi, Ghiberti and Donatello (the most famous names of the first half of the century, but there were many others) were all trained as goldsmiths, but turned their hands to sculpture or metalwork to make whatever a patron wanted.

Donatello pauses to explain a point, as his assistant refers to the sketches for the work and the young man who has been posing wraps up and comes to look. The statue is to be hollow (solid bronze would have been a waste of metal), so it is first modelled in clay. That stage is nearly complete.

Tubes to let bronze in and air out

To cast the statue, the clay model was first given a skin of wax. Details too fine to be made in clay were added in wax.

A coating of liquid clay was flicked on with a brush so that it filled every detail. Thicker clay went on top.

Clay lumps were added to make a huge mould which was held together with iron bands.

Wax rods from the figure came out of the top where bronze would go in later.

Some time probably in the 1440s Donatello made a bronze statue of the biblical hero David. It was remarkable in many ways: for its graceful realism, for its pose derived from classical sculpture and for the fact that it was naked apart from helmet and boots – the first large free-standing nude statue since classical times. Florentine artists were studying the beauty of the human body, a classical interest that medieval morality had firmly rejected. In the 15th century the statue stood in the courtyard of the Medicis' new palazzo, amid their prized ancient sculptures. It is now in the Bargello Museum, Florence.

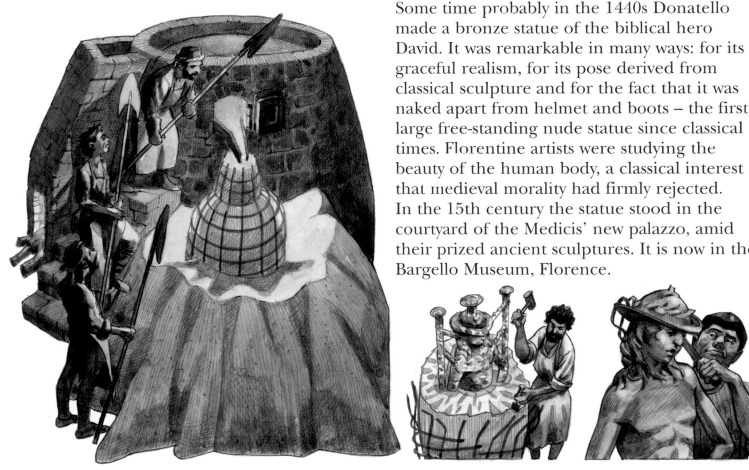

The mould was baked in a special oven. The wax skin and rods melted and ran out through holes in the bottom.

Molten metal was poured in through the holes left by the wax rods and filled everywhere the wax had been.

When the bronze-caster was sure that the metal was hard and cold, the clay casing was carefully chipped away.

The rods were sawn off and the clay model, now encased in bronze, was broken up and raked out through the base.

Fresco technique: a plasterer gives the wall its first coat, using a coarse plaster made of sand and lime.

To guide the artist a grid is marked out over the whole picture area, by snapping a chalked thread against the wall.

The artist transfers his design to the wall, following the grid. He outlines it with a brush and dark red paint.

Very fine plaster is put over a portion of the wall, but only as much as can be painted that day, while still wet.

Very rapidly the artist redraws the outlines of the design with red ochre. Then he indicates shadows with green.

Lighter tones and highlights are added last. If any plaster is left unpainted at the end of the day, it is cut away.

While assistants begin painting the landscape background, Benozzo Gozzoli shows Piero the whole design. A biblical subject was essential for a chapel, but the picture is really a celebration of the Medici family. They have prominent positions in the Magi's procession which winds through the Florentine countryside. The picture was done in fresco, a traditional technique for walls. The painting is done on damp plaster and is a great test of the artist's skill, as he must work fast and corrections are impossible.

Perspective is a technique for drawing solid objects on a flat surface so that they seem to be three-dimensional, exactly as the eye would see them. The rules of perspective are mathematical and are based on the way the eye receives light. Brunelleschi, who loved mathematical problems, made experiments which led him to discover perspective's rules.

Capturing Reality

Cosimo's palace took many years to complete. His son Piero, a great art lover, oversaw much of its decoration. In 1459 Piero engaged the painter Benozzo Gozzoli (1429–1497) to cover the chapel walls with a scene of the journey of the Magi (Wise Men). Gozzoli was just one among the amazing number of great painters in Florence in the 15th century. Botticelli (1444–1510), Leonardo da Vinci (1452–1519) and Michelangelo (1475–1564) were all Florentine artists.

A painter served a long apprenticeship as pupil-assistant to an established artist. He learnt how to grind and mix colours, how to draw by copying good pictures, and how to gild. When he was skilled enough he painted the easier parts in his master's work, copying his style. To these traditional skills Florentine artists added another: the mastery of perspective, which enables a draughtsman to represent space correctly. To medieval thinking, art existed to serve God, not to mirror reality, but the humanists gave a new value to things of this world. To them everything in it was interesting for its own sake. Florentine artists continued to paint religious pictures, but this world's beauty had a new importance for them. They wanted to capture its solidity, light and shade.

A WEDDING

Festivities in Florence were famous far and wide. Its artists produced spectacular ideas for public occasions – Leonardo once made a walking lion that opened to show a mass of lilies inside, and Brunelleschi designed ornaments for pageants.

Private celebrations could be very splendid, especially marriages between members of influential families. Such alliances made the families even richer and more powerful, and the bride's dowry – the money and possessions that went from her family to the groom's – was the most important point to settle, just as important as whether the bride and groom liked each other! Daughters of parents who could not raise a dowry often had to become nuns, as this was the only way of having a secure future.

When all was agreed, the betrothal took place. At that time weddings did not have to take place in church; a promise made before witnesses was binding. The Medici held a tournament (mock battle) to mark Lorenzo's betrothal to Clarice Orsini in 1469. Young men from all the leading families took part, wearing specially made armour and jewelled costumes. The feasting lasted for three days, with music, dancing, plays and five sumptuous banquets.

A wealthy bride arrives at her new home with her maids of honour. She is greeted with music and a shower of rose petals. After meeting her new family, the feasting will begin.

Good works

Even such a rich town as Florence had many poor citizens, too ill, old or unskilled to earn a living. If they had no family they had to rely on charity. Fortunately, the rich were very generous. Not only did the Church teach that charitable giving was a duty, it also insisted that charging interest on loans was sinful – and this gave many merchants a bad conscience. To put themselves right with God, they gave money to charities such as the hospital of Santa Maria Nuova, a home for orphans, and the confraternity of the Misericordia, which tended the sick and paid for funerals for the very poor.

Confraternities were societies formed by townsmen to do good works. The confraternity of Santa Maria della Pietà, founded in 1410 to help feed the poor, was typical. Members were expected to lead godly lives and attend Mass regularly. They met for prayers and society business. Some members prepared food for the poor and others gave it out. Surplus funds went to other good causes, such as paying for prisoners to be freed from gaol, but only if they had been 'imprisoned through misfortune, not through vice'.

Pilgrims are welcomed to a hostel by members of the confraternity that funds it. A white-aproned official has beds ready for them.

Unwanted children were cared for in the foundling hospital (below), designed by Brunelleschi. Right: a detail from the façade.

Feeding the hungry: confraternity members give poor citizens their allowance for the week.

The confraternity of Santa Maria della Pietà gave three loaves and a flask of wine to each.

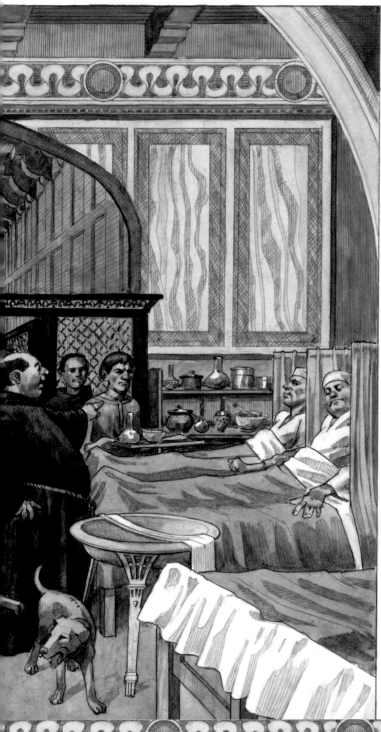

Providing clothes for the poor, or cloth to make them with, was also a charitable duty.

Charitable societies kept lists of needy people and records of what each one was given.

In a busy hospital ward (left), a doctor examines a patient. Hospitals served the poor and the care was free.

Visiting the homes of the sick (above) was another charitable task undertaken by the confraternities.

ENTERTAINMENTS

The Florentines were noted as hard workers, not likely to let slip the chance to make a profit, but when a holiday came they knew how to make the most of it. At festival times, houses and shopfronts were decorated with streamers and banners and people turned out in their finest clothes to watch the religious pageant with spectacular floats and scenery. Afterwards there was a tournament, a mock battle between wards (districts) of the city using wooden shields and poles, a *calcio* match (a type of football), or a hunt in the main square for which wild animals were let loose. There were parades and dancing, jugglers and stiltwalkers, torchlight processions and fireworks.

Almost all these holidays marked some important day in the Church calendar. In Florence the biggest celebrations were on 24 June, the feast of St John the Baptist, the town's patron saint. This was the day of the most magnificent processions and of the town's favourite sporting event, the *palio*, a bareback horse race through the streets, from one end of Florence to the other. The prize was a sumptuous banner (or *palio*) of gold-embroidered crimson silk, trimmed with fur and fringed with gold thread.

At the third stroke of the great bell in the Signoria, the jockeys hurtled down the streets, to frenzied shouts from the crowd.

Their mounts were the finest Barbary racehorses. Other towns had palios (Siena's is still held), and horses from outside Florence could be entered.

On the day of its patron saint, each town staged a huge procession. The scene above is taken from a 16th-century painting of the parade in the square at Siena.

Each ward of the town prepared a float in the shape of its emblem. Richly costumed ward representatives paraded behind each float, with banners flying.

THE TOWN AT WAR

The rivalry between Italian towns ensured that Florence was often at war with one or other of its neighbours. In theory all able-bodied citizens between the ages of 15 and 70 could be summoned to fight. In the past this had caused a lot of turmoil and prevented people from getting on with the serious business of making money. By the 14th century, Florence, like many other towns, was paying mercenaries (self-employed professional soldiers) to do its fighting for it. In order to have greater bargaining power, mercenaries banded together around a forceful leader. These men were called *condottieri*. (*Condottiere* is the singular).

Mercenaries were often foreigners – English, German or Hungarian – though by the 15th century Italians were taking over. Mercenaries had no loyalty to anyone but their condottiere, and he fought for any side that paid him. Condottieri were disliked. Many were suspected of dragging out campaigns to earn more, and of taking bribes. If they ran short of money for their men, they turned a blind eye while the men raided the countryside. But a few honest and respected condottieri were given honours and pensions. John Hawkwood, an English condottiere, served Florence on and off for over 20 years, becoming the town's permanent head of defence.

Hawkwood died in 1436 and the Signoria commissioned Paolo Uccello (1397–1475) to paint his portrait in the cathedral (left).

IOANNES·ACVTVS·EQVES·BRITANNICVS·DVX·AETATIS·S
VAE·CAVTISSIMVS·ET·REI·MILITARIS·PERITISSIMVS·HABITVS·E

The end of a siege: terms of surrender have been agreed and the victorious mercenaries march into the town.

Its inhabitants await them with dread. If the condottiere does not control his men, they may loot the town.

Gunpowder, introduced in the 14th century, meant that town walls had to support cannons and withstand their fire.

This posed mathematical design problems of a sort that appealed to Renaissance artists and architects. Brunelleschi, Leonardo da Vinci and Michelangelo all designed or supervised military fortifications.

TOWN & COUNTRY

The Florentines had close ties with the country. Noble families owned castles there, and many town families had been farm workers a few generations earlier. A successful citizen often bought a farm near the town. Worked by peasants who shared in the profits, it kept his family in food and was a pleasant place to visit. Prosperous citizens had one or two farms; rich merchants had several country villas with large estates.

At his villa a merchant could go hunting and hawking like an aristocrat, or dirty his hands pruning vines and weeding, as Cosimo de' Medici did. The villa was a place to escape from business, to study and discuss ideas with a few close friends.

A year's country tasks, from plaques by Luca della Robbia: January, cutting wood; February, grafting fruit trees.

March, pruning old growth from the vines; April, bending down the new shoots and tying them in place.

May, cutting the first of the hay. June, a busy month; wheat, oats and beans are harvested, and hay is cut again.

July, threshing corn to beat the grain from the ears; August, ploughing harvested fields ready for autumn sowing.

September, picking grapes. Sound bunches are cut from the vine. October, sowing grain for next year's harvest.

November, harvesting olives for pickling and for making into oil; December, digging uncultivated ground.

Only townspeople see country life as one of leisure and freedom from care. In the Middle Ages feudal lords and peasants had thought of it as a workplace. But in ancient Rome, people in public life had craved for the peace of the country and written of their love of fine views, pure air and solitude. The Florentines of the Renaissance who studied their writings responded to this. At their villas they felt they were recreating the ideal life of the classical world. They imitated classical poems in praise of country life. This attitude has had an enormous influence on people's feelings about the countryside ever since.

This is the villa of the Medici estate at Caffagiolo, north of Florence. It is still there, minus its central tower. Cosimo de' Medici inherited the land in 1451 and probably built the villa. Lorenzo spent much of his childhood here. The building looks rather like a fortress, with machicolated towers, a moat and drawbridge – signs that the countryside was not always a peaceful place.

41

November 1515: Pope Leo X, Giovanni de' Medici, crosses the city square on his way to the cathedral. In front of the Pope, the Holy Sacrament is carried on a white mare whose bridle and blanket are embroidered with pearls.

THE TOWN TRIUMPHANT

In 1513, Florence heard news that sent everyone in the town wild with joy. A Florentine had been elected Pope. Cardinal Giovanni de' Medici, son of Lorenzo, had become Pope Leo X. For three days the bells were rung. Bonfires blazed – in some places, celebrating youths went on the rampage, tearing down roofs and doors. The Medici showered money from their palace windows and distributed wine and food in the streets.

In 1515 the Pope came to Florence and the Signoria prepared a magnificent display in his honour: the greatest spectacle the town had ever seen. Two thousand men worked to make the decorations that lined the route of his triumphal procession.

The festival brought together, in one majestic display, the town's magnificently robed nobles and leading citizens, its military companies and its clergy. Thousands marched to music and cheering. The people of Florence watched from doorways, windows and rooftops, their hearts swelling with pride.

The people of the town were right to feel triumphant. Florence's achievements were famous far and wide. All over Italy, ideas that had spread from the city were prompting people to experiment in architecture, painting, sculpture and writing. It would not be long before these ideas were carried over the Alps to the rest of Europe.

CHRONOLOGY OF FLORENCE

59 BC The Romans establish a colony, Florentia, beside the Arno. The Via Torta (Crooked Street) in modern Florence still follows the curve of Florentia's amphitheatre.

AD

5th century Florentia surrenders to the Goths who are overrunning Italy.

570 New invaders, the Lombards, create a dukedom which controls what little remains of Florentia.

825 The Emperor Lothair starts an ecclesiastical school in Florence. The town slowly regains prestige.

1059 The baptistery, parts of which date from the 5th or 6th century, is restored and reconsecrated.

12th century Though officially ruled by the Holy Roman Emperor, Florence is self-ruling. The walls are rebuilt to enclose a larger area.

13th century The wool industry develops.

1284–1333 An even wider circuit of walls is built to accommodate the population of around 100,000.

1293 The Florentine constitution is established, making the guilds the representatives of the people. Trade booms and Florence is at the height of its commercial prosperity.

1294 Work begins on the new cathedral of Santa Maria del Fiore, designed by Arnolfo di Cambio.

1299 The building of the Palace of the Signoria begins.

1334 The bell tower of the cathedral is begun, to a design by Giotto.

1348 The Black Death kills nearly 60 per cent of Florence's inhabitants.

1360s Petrarch is discussing classical authors with his friends.

1375–1406 Coluccio Salutati, a friend of Petrarch, is Chancellor of Florence and encourages classical studies.

1378	Discontented cloth workers rebel. They control the Signoria for four years.
1396	Coluccio Salutati invites Manuel Chrysoloras, the Byzantine scholar, to Florence to teach Greek.
1397	Giovanni di Bicci de' Medici sets up the headquarters of the Medici banking business in Florence.
1402	Ghiberti wins the competition for making bronze doors for the baptistery.
c.1402	Brunelleschi and Donatello go to Rome.
c.1410–1430	Niccolò Niccoli, a Florentine scholar who inherited a fortune made in the wool industry, spends so much on rare manuscripts that he becomes bankrupt.
1419–1420	Brunelleschi's design for the cathedral dome is approved. He discovers the laws of perspective.
1421	Giovanni di Bicci de' Medici begins the Medici patronage of art by commissioning Brunelleschi to build a sacristy for the Medici parish church of San Lorenzo.
c.1425–1427	The young painter Masaccio astounds Florence with the perspective effect of his fresco of the Holy Trinity in the church of Santa Maria Novella.
1428	Masaccio dies at the age of 27 – the greatest Italian painter of his age.
1429	Cosimo de' Medici inherits an immense fortune on his father's death. He collects manuscripts and funds Niccolò Niccoli's collecting.
1436	The new cathedral is consecrated by Pope Eugenius IV.
1436–1443	Cosimo finances the rebuilding of the Dominican monastery and library of San Marco, to designs by Michelozzo.

1437	Niccolò Niccoli dies. His manuscripts enter Cosimo's collection, which he allows scholars to study. It later becomes the first public library in Europe.
1439	Due to Cosimo's diplomacy, a meeting between the Pope and a delegation from the Greek Orthodox Church, accompanied by the Byzantine emperor, is held in Florence. For many weeks Florentine and Greek scholars mix.
1446–1460	The Palazzo Medici is built.
1453	Constantinople (capital of the Byzantine empire) is captured by the Turks. Many Byzantine scholars flee to Italian cities, bringing Greek manuscripts with them.
1464	Death of Cosimo de' Medici.
1469	Cosimo's son Piero dies, and the Florentines ask Lorenzo, Piero's 20-year-old son, to lead them.
c.1469–1476	The young Leonardo is an apprentice painter in Florence.
c.1475	Botticelli's *Adoration of the Magi* honours the Medici as patrons by including portraits of the three generations of the family.
1478	The Pazzi, a Florentine family hostile to the Medici, try to overthrow them by attempting to murder Lorenzo and his brother during a service in the cathedral. Lorenzo escapes; his brother is killed.
1492	Death of Lorenzo.
1494–1559	Charles VIII of France invades Italy, beginning a series of wars between foreign and Italian states. When the invaders return to northern Europe, they take Renaissance ideas with them.
1503	Leonardo paints a large mural in the council Chamber of the Palace of the Signoria.
1513	Leo X is the first Medici Pope.
1519–1532	Michelangelo sculpts the monuments to the Medici in their chapel in San Lorenzo.
1531	The Holy Roman Emperor makes Alessandro de' Medici duke of Florence. Medici dukes rule until 1737.

GLOSSARY

Academy In the 15th-century sense, a group of scholars meeting informally. The name comes from a park in ancient Athens where the philosopher Plato talked with his pupils.

Apothecary A seller of medicines, spices and sweetmeats.

Apprentice A young person who works for a master, and in return is taught the master's trade.

Baptistery A building next to, or a chamber within, a church, where baptism takes place.

Bust A statue representing the head and shoulders of a person.

Byzantium An eastern Mediterranean empire with its capital at Constantinople (modern Istanbul). It was all that was left of the eastern half of the Roman empire and was destroyed by the Turks in 1453.

Choirloft A balcony in a church from which the choir sings.

Curfew A regulation that, after a certain time in the evening, people must stay indoors.

Etruscans A people who flourished in central Italy from the 8th century BC. In the 5th century BC their influence declined and they were later overcome by the Romans.

Façade The front of a building.

Feud A long-lasting fight or dispute between different families or groups.

Feudal Belonging to a system of government called feudalism, in which lords or knights were given land by their overlord, and had to serve the overlord in return.

Forum A central open space in a Roman town around which official buildings were grouped.

Foundling An abandoned baby cared for by charity.

Fulling The process of cleaning and thickening newly woven cloth by beating and washing it.

Gilding Covering a surface with very thin sheets of gold.

Grafting Inserting a shoot from a plant into a slit in the stem of a stronger, coarser one. The shoots of the host plant are cut back, so its roots feed the grafted shoot.

Herald A person who makes official announcements.

Holy Sacrament In the Roman Catholic faith, the mystical transformation of bread and wine into the body and blood of Christ.

Horn of plenty A container in the shape of a goat's horn, overspilling with flowers, fruit and corn.

Humanist A Renaissance scholar interested in the revival of classical learning. The term comes from *studia humanitatis*, the study of the arts – literature, history and rhetoric (the art of speaking). Universities still call arts subjects 'the humanities'.

Lantern The architectural term for a small construction with glazed sides, projecting from a dome, or the ceiling of a room or stairwell, to let light in.

Loggia An arcade with one or more sides open.

Machicolated Provided with an overhanging parapet or upper storey, the floor of which has openings through which weapons, such as molten lead and stones, can be dropped.

Manuscript A text written by hand.

Medallion A large medal – a decorative metal disc bearing a portrait or an inscription.

Niche A recess in a wall, usually to hold a statue.

Overlord A lord who has power over other lords or states.

Overseer A person who supervises other people at work.

Pagan Belonging to a religion which is not related to Judaism, Christianity or Islam.

Palazzo (plural **palazzi**) A large, rich town house.

Patron A person who commissions work from artists or supports them with money.

Plaque A ceramic or metal ornamental tablet intended to hang on or be inset in a wall.

Plato A Greek philosopher (*c.*427–*c.*347 BC) and one of the most influential figures in Western civilisation. His philosophy was taught until AD 529 when the Emperor Justinian, a Christian, closed the pagan schools of philosophy. Plato's thought has influenced Christian, Jewish and Islamic philosophical traditions.

Relief A surface carved or moulded so that a pattern or figures project from it.

Republic A state whose leaders are chosen by vote.

Sarcophagus (plural **sarcophagi**) A stone coffin.

Trucklebed A low bed on wheels, stowed away during the day.

Villa A large country house, usually the centre of a farming estate.

INDEX